Dedicated to our parents:

Juanita & Maceo Nelson and
Edna & Fletcher Galloway.

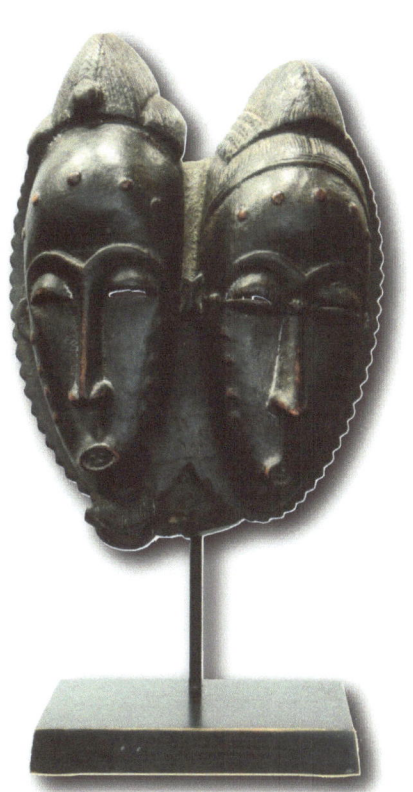

ChristopherHealth.com

Special thanks to
Kijana Wiseman-Fusilier, M.Ed.
for design and the addition of African proverbs

&

Clive Richardson
for artwork photography

"Knowledge is like a garden.
If it is not cultivated, it cannot be harvested"

-African proverb from Guinea

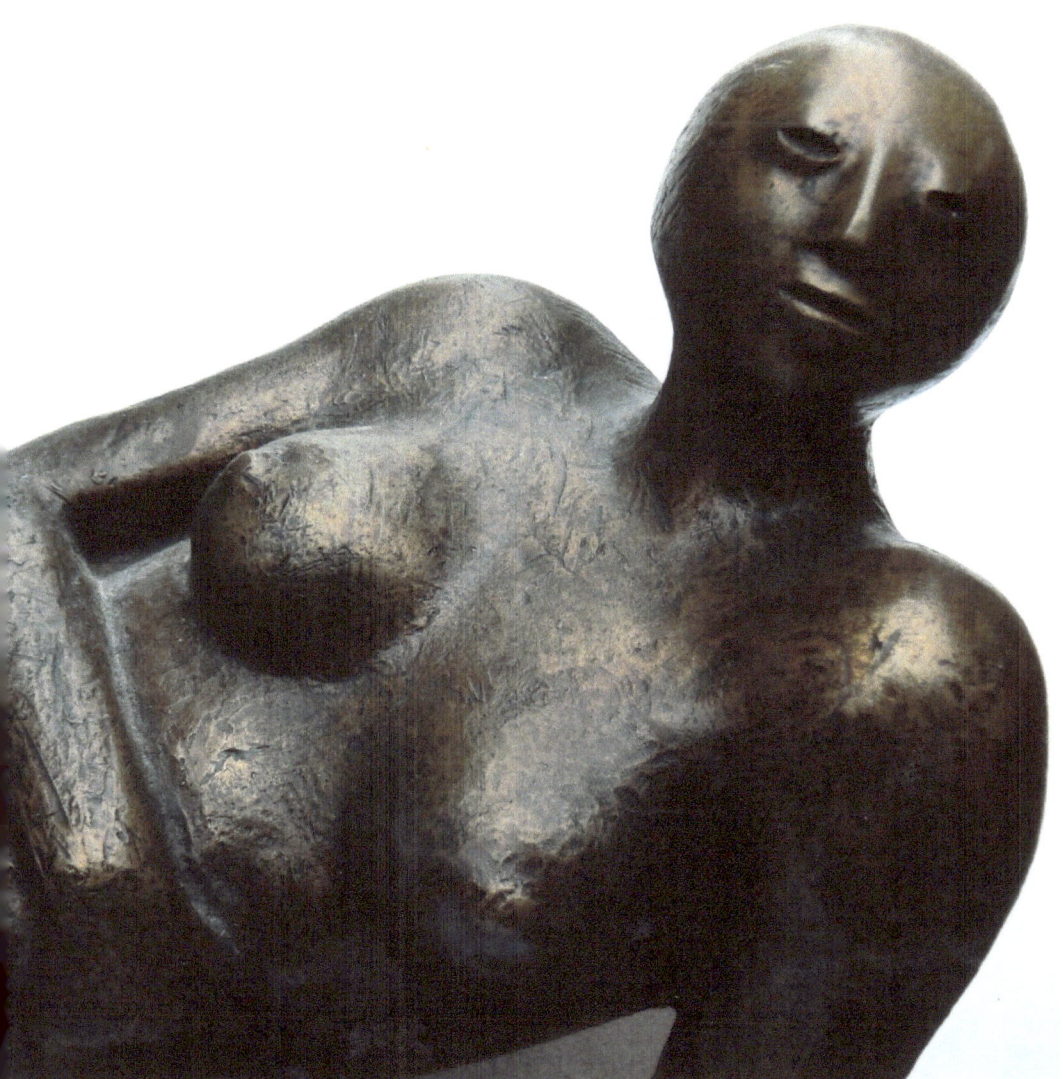

"Reclining Woman"

A bronze sculpture by
Elizabeth Catlett

"*Yombe*"

Foreword:

Discovering Woman...

The essential part of my being at present, is based upon two women; my mother, Edna Branch Galloway, who was born in a little town in Brookshire, Texas, and my wife, Jean Nelson Galloway, who was born in Charleston, West Virginia. Both gave me unconditional love at those times when I needed to express the importance of the growth of my soul and to continue the process of maturation.

My mother was the eldest of her clan, so that when her younger sister ran off to Chicago, it was her job to go and fetch her. Shortly after arrival to Chicago, my mom met and married this handsome man from Yazoo, Mississippi. That was my dad, Fletcher Galloway and so my mom didn't come back to Brookshire for a while. That's where I was born. As the years rolled by my mom insisted that I spend my summers in Brookshire. I cooperated, even though I didn't understand her reasoning. When I grew older and more mature I recognized her wisdom, for many of my friends in Chicago got into trouble over the summers.

As I became older, I incorporated the cultures of the south with the north and I became stronger. I considered this, along with an indomitable mother and father, as a huge blessing from God and my foundation.

My mother had aspired to be a doctor when she was younger, but was unable to do so because of America's Jim Crow obstacles. So she sent me instead.

While studying Medicine at Yale School of Medicine in New Haven, Connecticut, I paused to accept a summer externship at the University of the West Indies in Kingston, Jamaica. There, I studied sickle cell anemia in the days, but in the evenings I listened to the reggae musicians singing songs of Ethiopian kings/ prophets/ gods, and I pondered the connection with other African cultures. The lyrics and their mystery faded, but continued to haunt me after I returned to America. I continued my studies and eventually was accepted at the Case-Western Reserve University in Cleveland, Ohio to do my residency in Internal Medicine. That's where I met my wife who was also studying medicine.

We became friends and dated. At the same time my research interests in tropical Infectious diseases increased so I solidified a research project in Ethiopia (Where I had secretly wanted to go to since Jamaica). So in July of 1974 --with the support of the National Institutes of Health in Bethesda, Maryland, Johns Hopkins University, and Case Western Reserve-- I left for Addis Ababa, Ethiopia, to do my research. As an aside, I saw confirmation of the ancient legends hinted at by those musical lyrics years earlier in Jamaica. Later, while traveling along the Blue Nile River, I saw obelisks with hieroglyphics, ancient tombs, and proud people. Although these people were materially poor, they were wealthy because of their awareness of their history. Inscriptions written over many of the ancients tombs, said "KNOW THYSELF." This too would continue to haunt me like the old lyrics from Jamaica. I traveled through Kenya, Tanzania, and Uganda to the Nile Rift Valley. The latter, according to Dr. Louis Leakey, was the cradle of

Civilization. The discovery of these ancient and significant cultures was an epiphany of inspiration for me.

I returned to America, and to Houston, Texas where I had left Jean, the love of my life. If there were any significance to the refrain "KNOW THYSELF" then this was it. A strong intuitive sense told me that man was a spiritual being and this lady was my soulmate. Therefore the right thing to do was to ask her to marry me. I did and she said…."YES."

In the mid 1970s. I met and became close friends with Dr. John Biggers. Dr. Biggers was a world famous artist who founded the Art Department at Texas Southern University. I was impressed with the depth and breath of his works. He taught me the

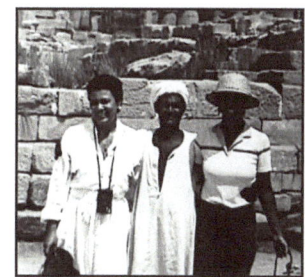

Jean Galloway and Akua McDaniels with a Nubian Guide in Egypt
(Photo: Robert. Galloway)

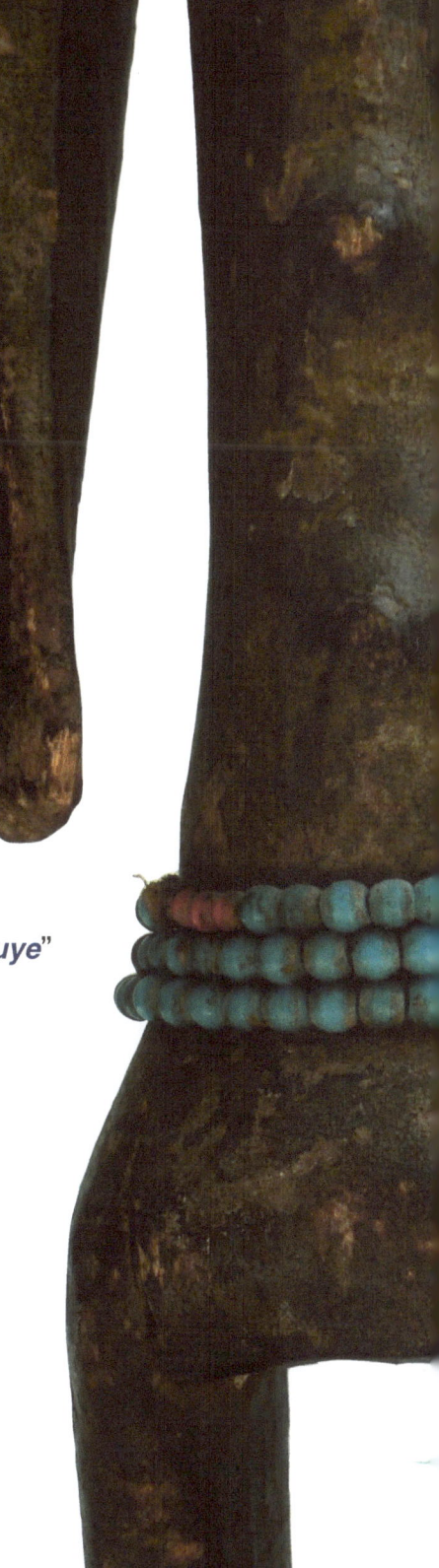

"Mumuye"

rich symbolism in African art and convinced me that the keys and language for understanding ancestral wisdom resided within traditional African sculptured forms. This became my passion. Slowly, I began collecting as it appeared to be synonymous with the spirit of my ancestral legacy.

in 1984, Jean and I arrived in Egypt with Dr. Asa Hilliard III, an egyptologist and archeologist of distinction. With us was Dr. Lois O. Williams Hilliard (mother of Dr. Hilliard) and Akua McDaniel, Chair of the Art Department at Spelman College (and my wife's best friend).

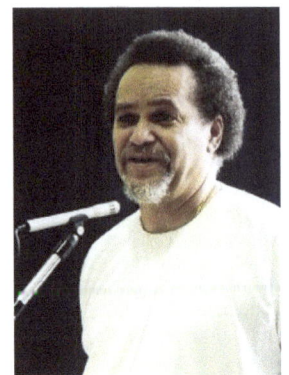

Egyptologist Asa Hilliard
(Photo courtesy of the Hilliard Family

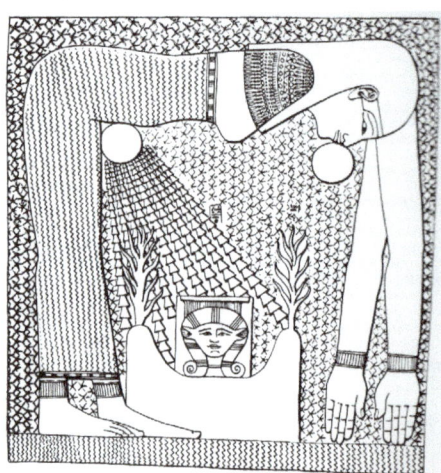

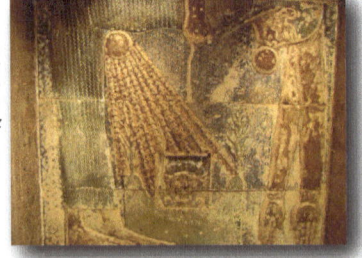

Graphic renderings of the Egyptian goddess Nut as illustrated by Lucie Lamy and published in "Her-Bak: The Living Face of Ancient Egypt" and "Her-Bak: Egyptian Initiate" by Isha Shwaller De Lubicz

(© 1954, Inner Traditions Ltd)

We traveled with 51 other Americans from Cairo through lower and upper Egypt to Sudan/ Nubia, exploring numerous pyramids and obelisks with hieroglyphs.

After Luxor, we went to Abydos, Egypt. There, we saw the Goddess Nut (pronounced "Noot"), whose entire body--representing the universe--was painted on the ceiling of a temple. She was massive, covering the entire room: with stars surrounding her; the sun emerging from her mouth and the moon at her womb with a cradled infant beneath it.

Outside the temple were obelisks which were towering phallic structures representing the masculine principle. There were also pyramids that represented the natural motive force which sustains and directs the world; feminine principle.

The obelisk and pyramid together as Unity symbolically embrace the totality of life. This concept is wonderfully illustrated at Houston's Menil Museum. The reflecting pool outside the museum's Rothko Chapel hosts "The Broken Obelisk" a sculpture by Barnett Newman, commissioned by the DeMenils as a memorial to Dr. Martin Luther King, Jr.

Dr. King delivered his "I Have a Dream" speech, speech in Washington, D.C. on the steps of the Lincoln Memorial. In the distance, he could see the most impressive obelisk in America, the "Needle." He was later assassinated and therefore never saw his dream fulfilled...the obelisk remained broken.

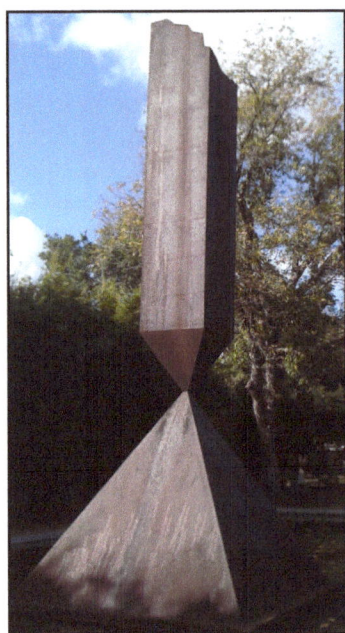

The Broken Obelisk at the Menil Museum in Houston, Texas
(Photo: Robert Galloway)

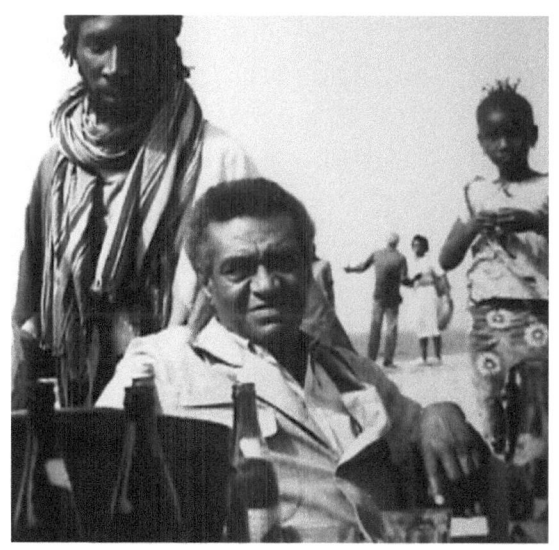

Dr. John Biggers on Goreé Island, Senegal, West Africa
(Photo: Robert. Galloway)

We envision this book to serve as an inspiration to young people--especially young women-- empowering them to recognize their potential early in life by embracing the meaning of "KNOW THYSELF." Our ultimate goal is to help maximize the human potential by incorporating the knowledge presented here into school curriculums as a teaching tool for educators.

This journey has been both long and purposeful in rediscovering the sacred unity of life itself. My appreciation for both my mother and wife has been extended to an understanding that the universe evolves around Man's appreciation for the role Woman plays in the evolution and connectivity of the universe.

Dr. Robert Galloway

In 1986, Jean and I took our son, Todd Christopher Galloway, to Dakar, Senegal. We were accompanied by John and Hazel Biggers and about two hundred travelers from North and South America. While there, we visited Goree' Island the port from which, during the 18th century, millions of distressed human souls had been kidnapped, tagged and stolen on ships bound for the Americas. I resonated with their pain, the rhythm of the land, the ocean, the village, and the marketplace—some of the items I collected there are presented here.

The Human Genome Project demonstrated in 2003, that all humans have a common African heritage, based on the early research of Dr. Louis Leakey, a Kenyan archaeologist and anthropologist.

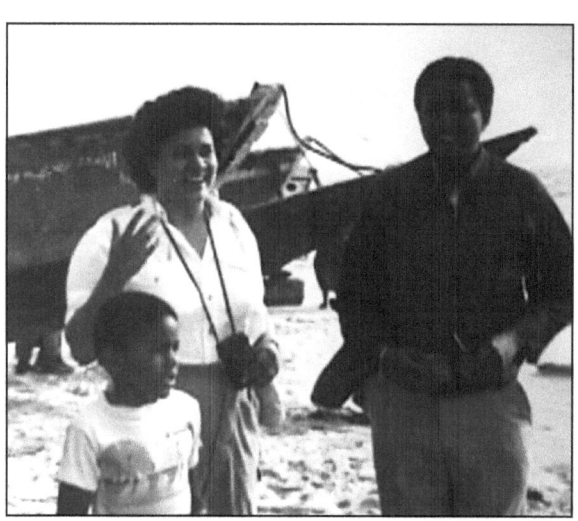

Jean Galloway, Amadou Niang and young Todd Christopher Galloway in Senegal.
(Photo: Robert Galloway)

Hand-painted Parchment Certificate / Cartouche

Dr. Asa Hilliard awarded this valuable hand-crafted papyrus scroll to each of us, authenticating the completion of his course of study. The certificate measures 16x14 inches with the recipient's name inscribed on the left margin. All 51 students received this document at the end of the course.

The Name of the Recipient is in Ancient Hieroglyphics

The name of the recipient is written in the left hand margin of each of the certificates in English and in the center in ancient hieroglyphics.

The Cartouche

In Egyptian hieroglyphs, a cartouche is an ellipse with a horizontal line at one end, indicating that the text enclosed is a royal name.
(Source: Wikipedia.com

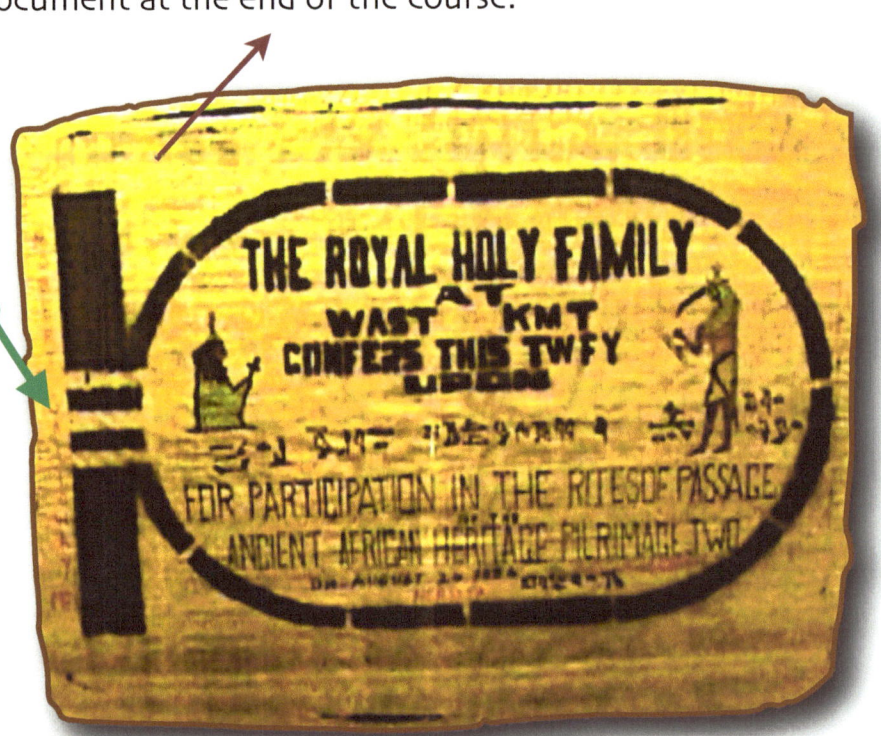

Robert Galloway's Certificate

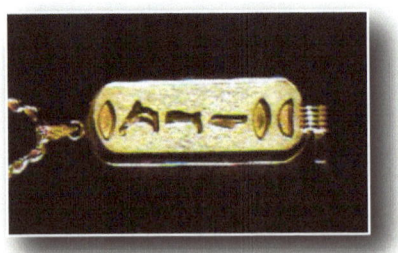

Robert Galloway's name engraved in gold on cartouche pendant.

Jean Galloway's Certificate

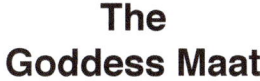

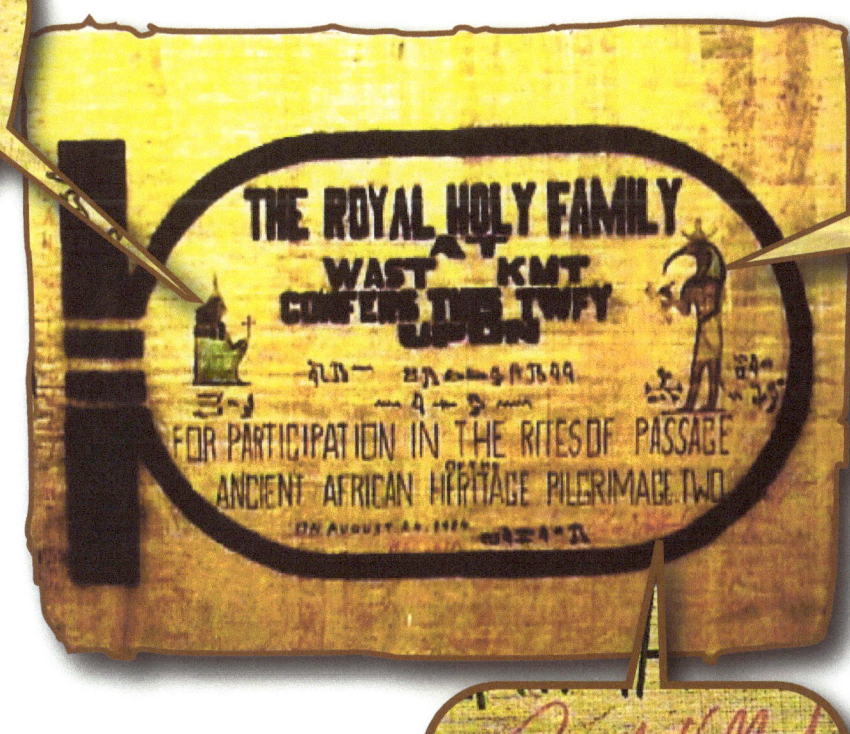

THE ROYAL HOLY FAMILY AT WAST KMT CONFERS THIS TWFY UPON

FOR PARTICIPATION IN THE RITES OF PASSAGE ANCIENT AFRICAN HERITAGE PILGRIMAGE TWO

ON AUGUST 4, 1994

The Goddess Maat

Maat is the Egyptian goddess of truth and justice.

The God Thoth

Thoth is the Egyptian god of thought and consciousness.

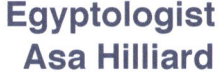

Egyptologist Asa Hilliard

(Photo courtesy of the Hilliard Family

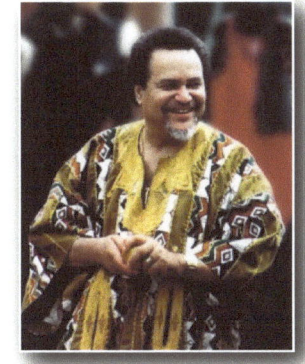

Asa Hilliard's Signature

Each certificate was individually signed by Egyptologist Asa Hilliard .

"Children are the reward of life"

-African proverb from Zaire

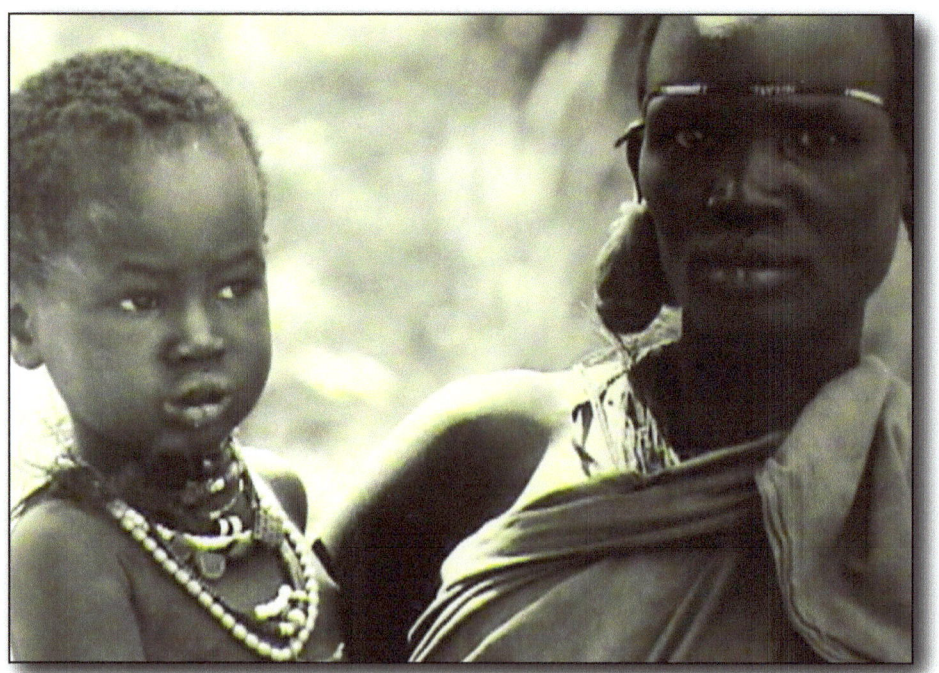

A Gambella woman and child in Ethiopia
(Photo: Robert Galloway, 1st Place Winner at Houston PhotoFest)

"A man's wealth may be superior to him"

-African proverb from Cameroon

Baule Mother and Child

A mother and child sculpture in very old Ivory (noticed the multiple cracks of age.). The tribe is Baule. From the front, one can see the third eye indicating a very high center of consciousness. A beautiful coiffeur and numerous tribal markings indicate that this is based on an advanced language and system of thought.

Coming around the sides are tiny hands of a baby. The mother is holding the seat of the baby. She is the foundation of all civilization and life on earth.

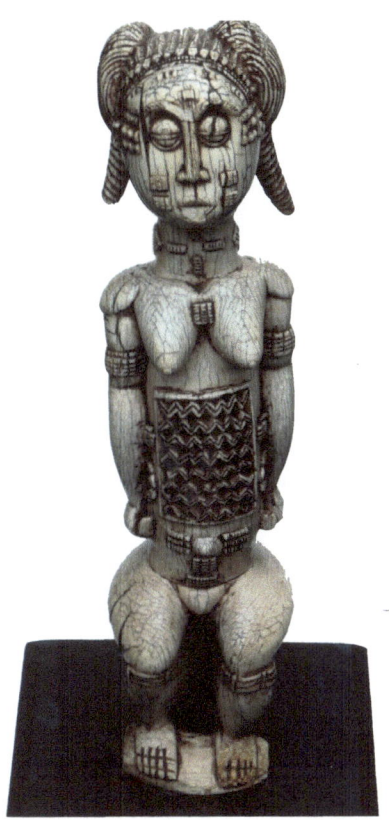

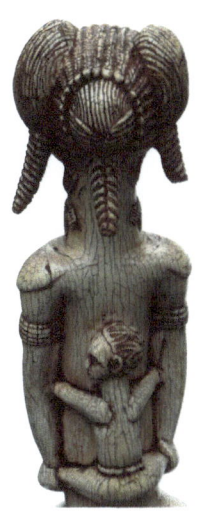

This view shows the baby. The woman is the only way in which men can create. The mother's braid of hair points to her creation.

Antique ivory, the most valued and precious material, is used to show the most important possession of a man--his wife and offspring.

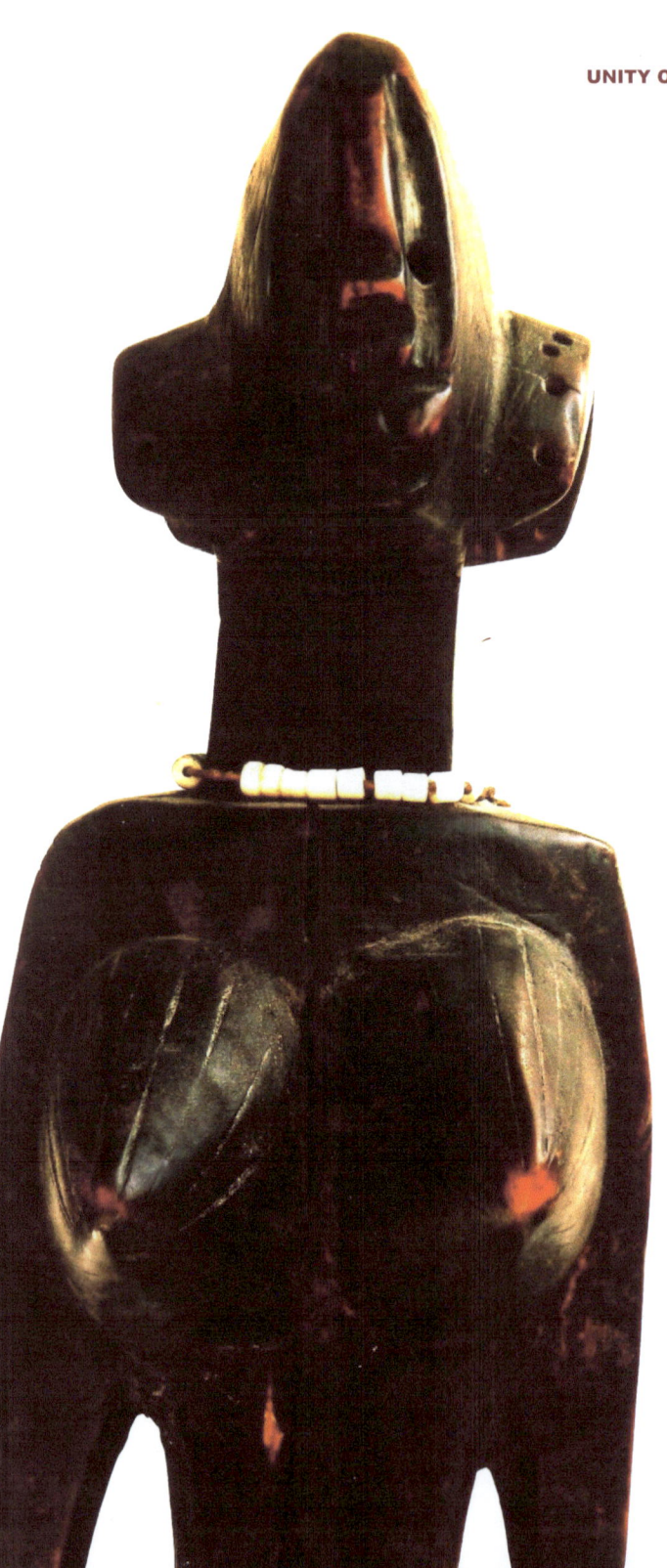

"No matter how full the river,
it stills continues to grow"

-African proverb from Zaire

Bamana Woman

Notice the full breasts
denoting an abundance
of nurturing.

"A little subtleness is better than a lot of force"

-African proverb from Zaire

A Yoruba Mother

A Yoruba woman and child kneeling and demonstrating one of the highest of human virtues--generosity--as manifested by the giving of food in the form of a chicken to a stranger.

She is royalty as manifested by her hairdo which is shaped like the crown of a pharaoh. She also has the third eye, a symbol of her heightened consciousness.

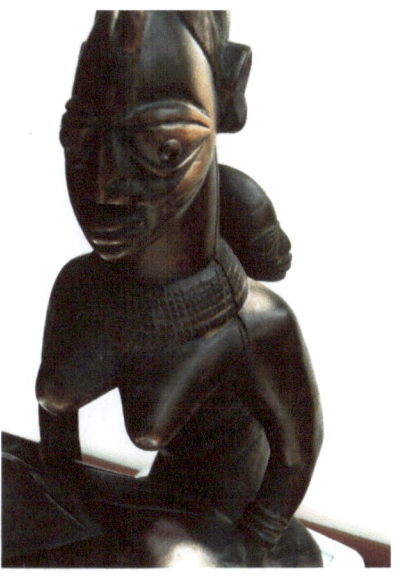

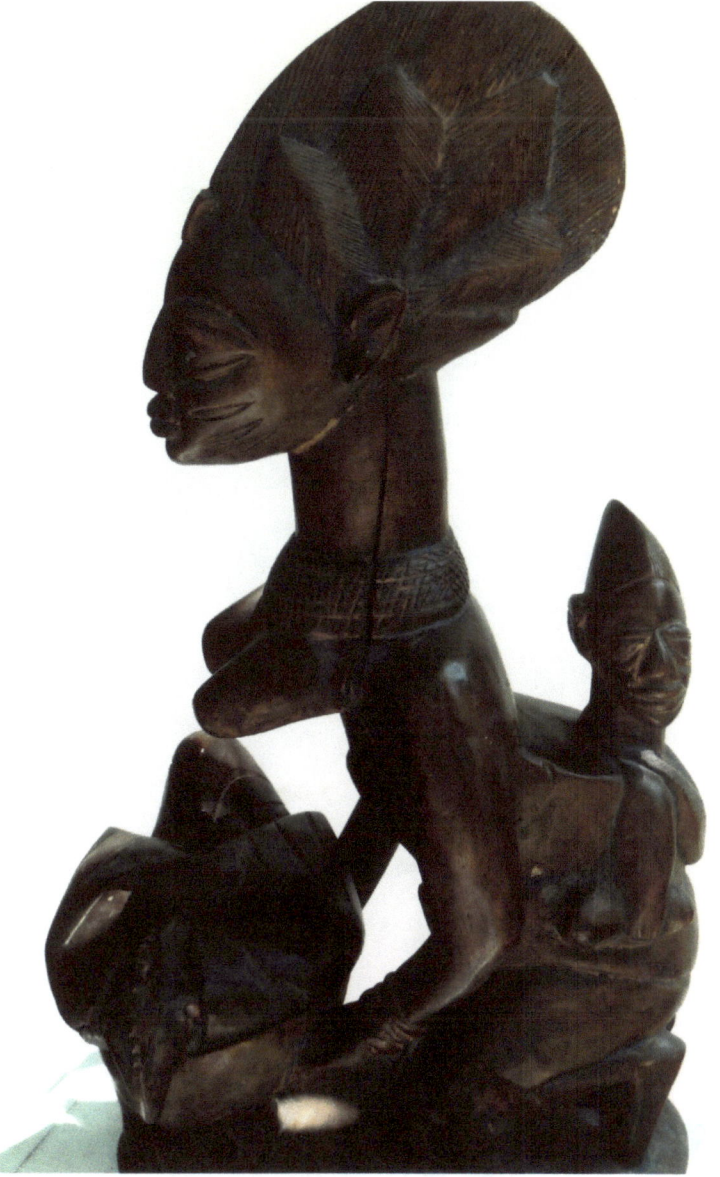

13

"He who is unable to dance.
says the yard is stoney"

-African proverb from Kenya

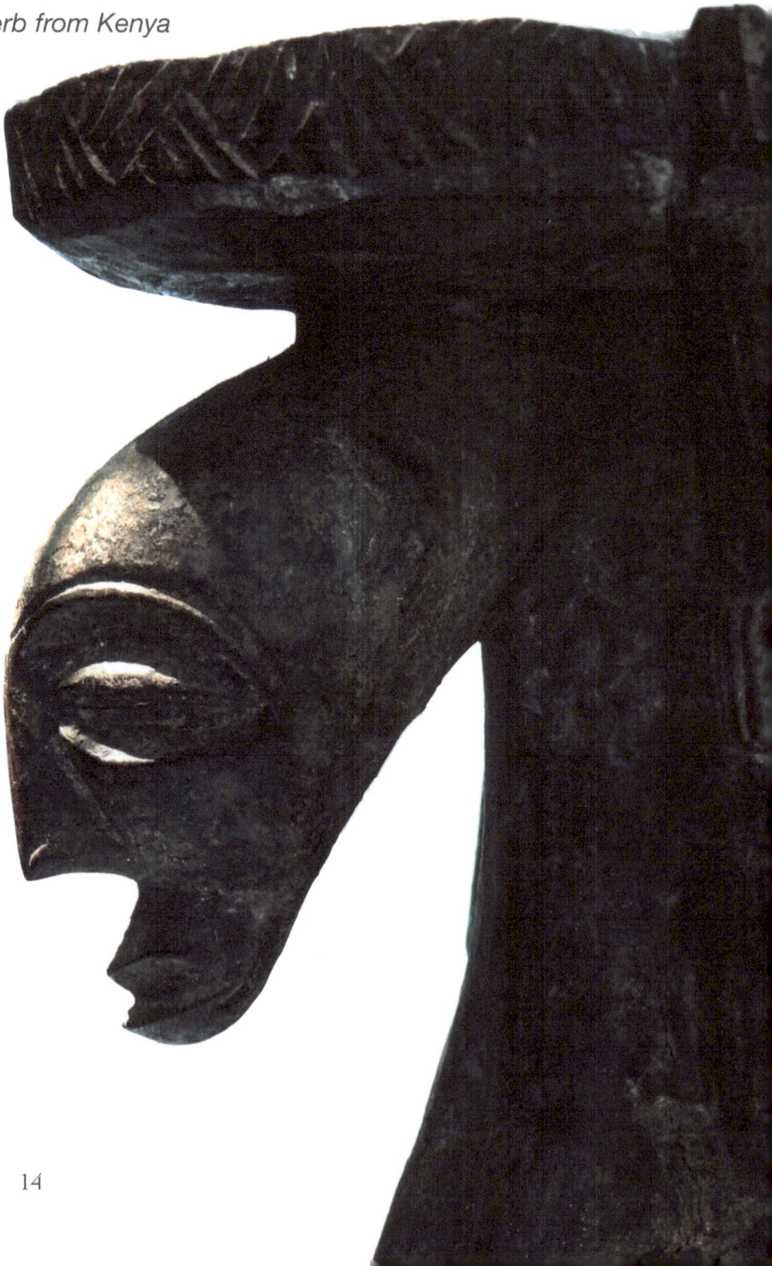

A Luba Woman Stool

A Luba stool, showing a
majestic woman's face.
This angular style is
undoubtedly the source of
the original inspiration of
Picasso and Matisse.

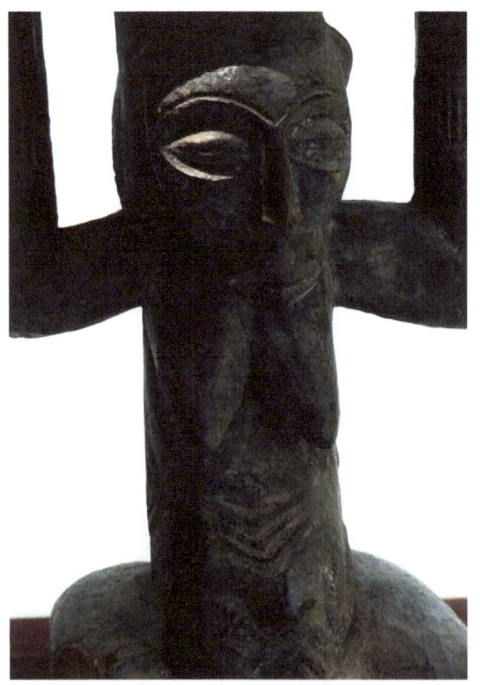

"He who does not cultivate his field
will die of hunger"

-African proverb from Ghana

**Yombe Mother
and Child**

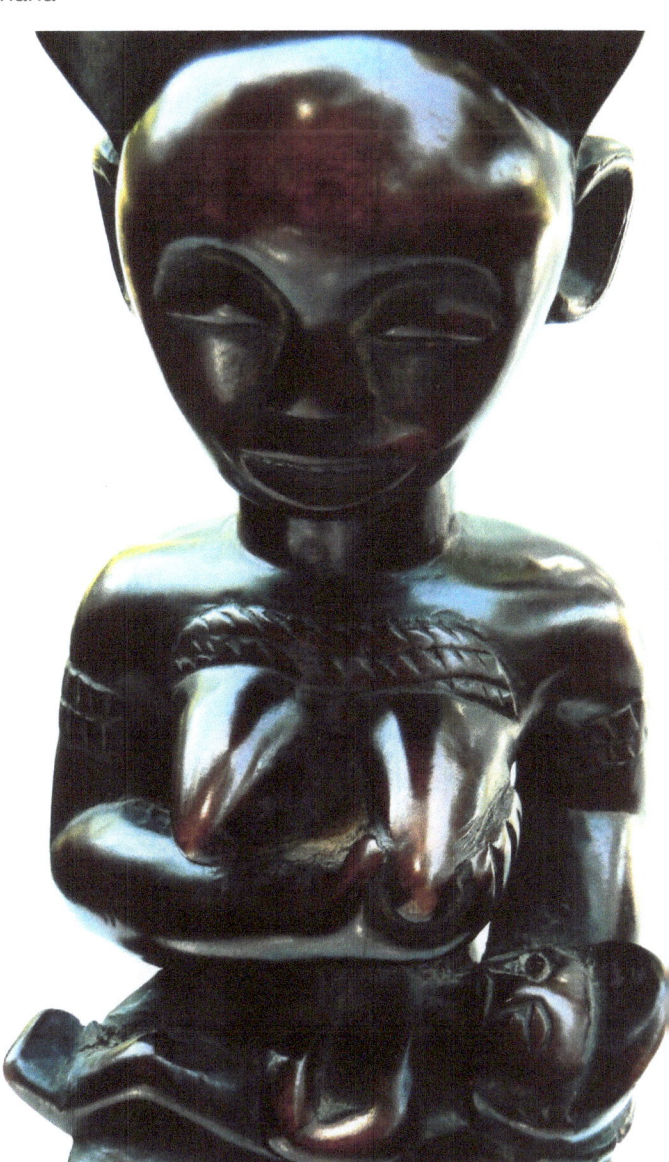

15

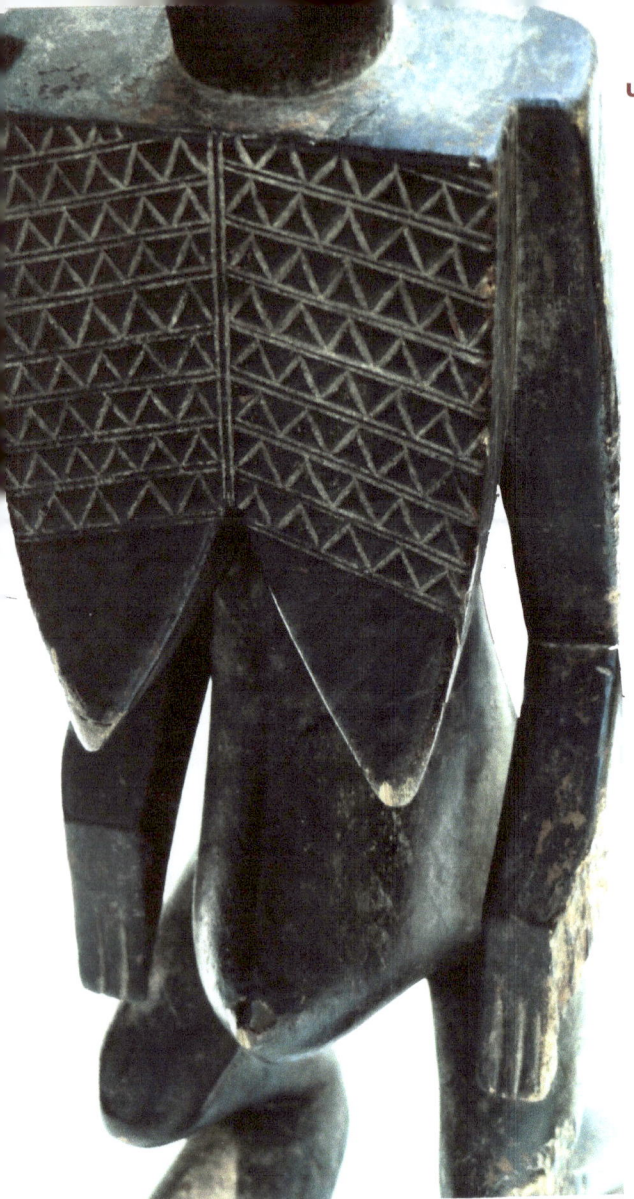

"Around a flowing tree
one finds many insects."

-African proverb from Guinea

Bambara Majesty

This Bambara statue
proudly displays her large
beautiful breasts.

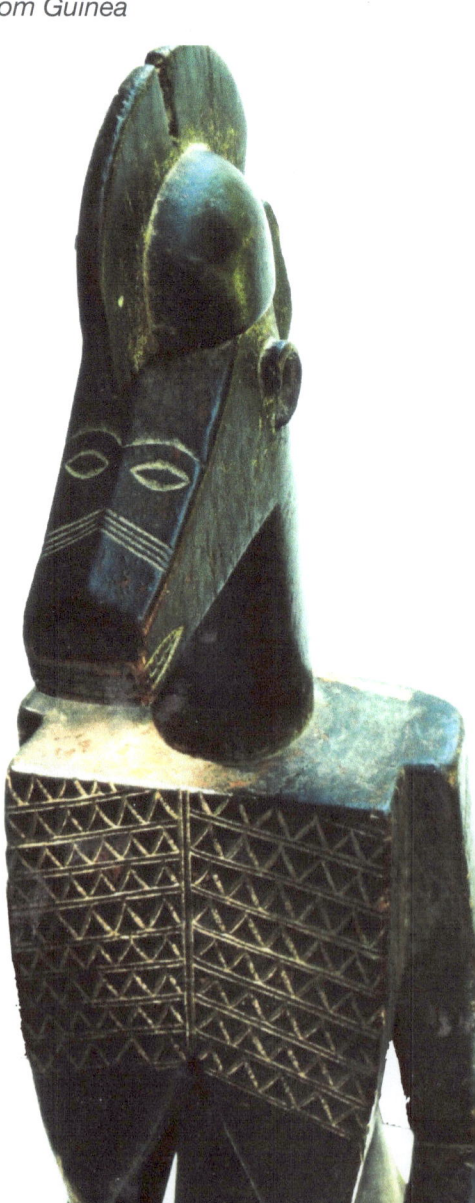

Again, the cubism
captured by Picasso is
born here.

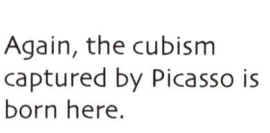

16

"When one is in love, a cliff becomes a meadow"

-African proverb from Ethiopia

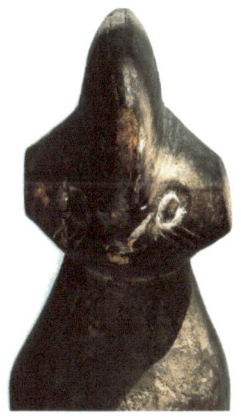

Mumuye Woman
(in two parts)

This Mumuye statue appears to have two umbilical cords, suggesting that we are connected to two different worlds at different stages of our lives.

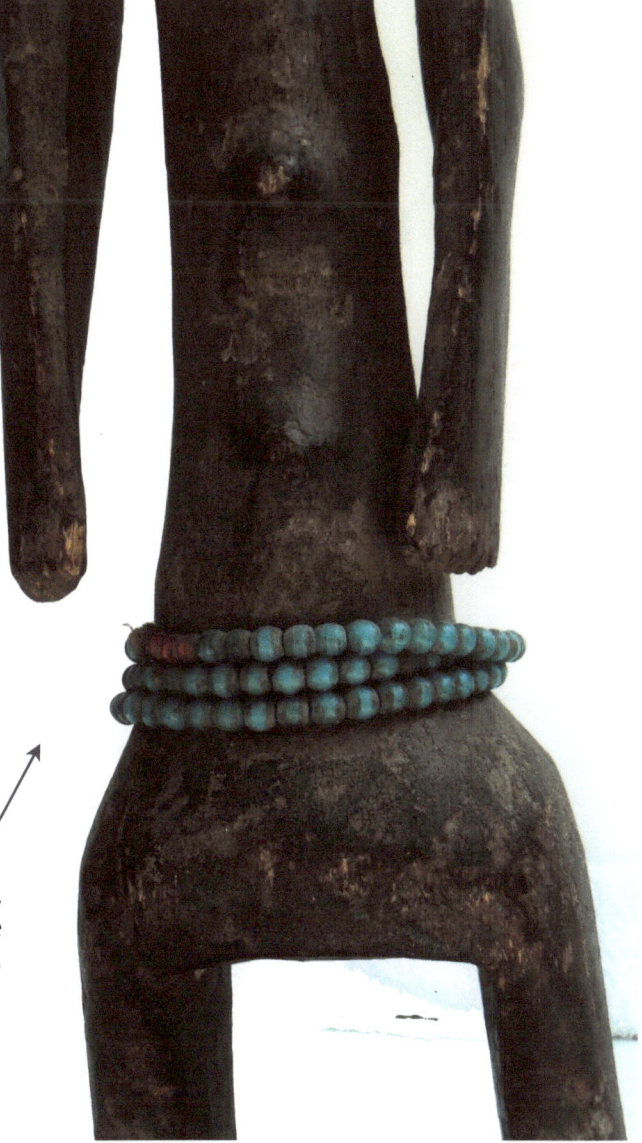

These are fertility beads, designed to encourage procreation.

17

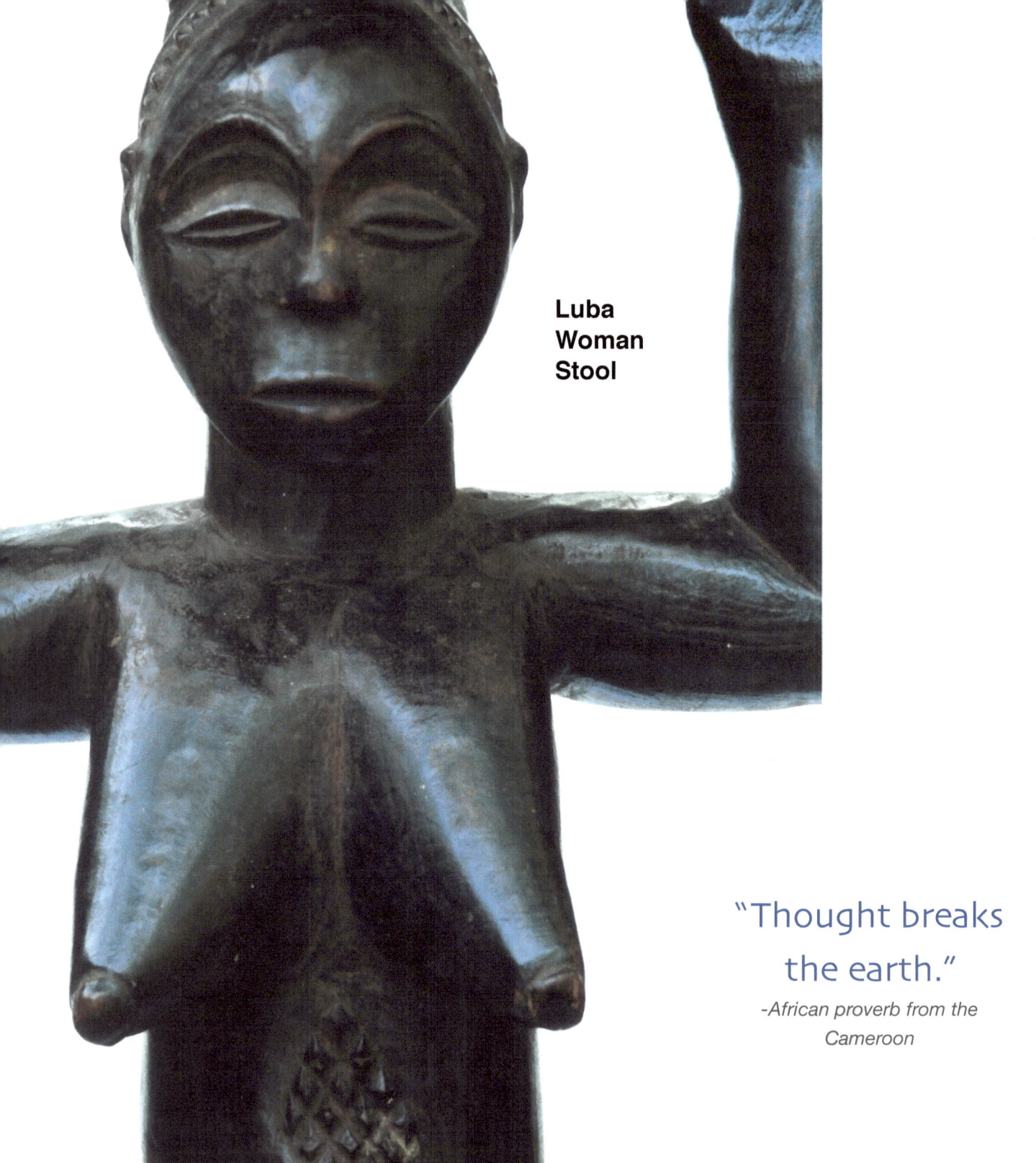

**Luba
Woman
Stool**

"Thought breaks
the earth."

-African proverb from the
Cameroon

"Where there is no shame there is no honor"

-African proverb from Ethiopia

Two Vases: Yin & Yang

These vases from China show
the influence of African art on the world.

The female (Yin) is the feminine element.
Here, the gentleness of the female
is represented by the bird.

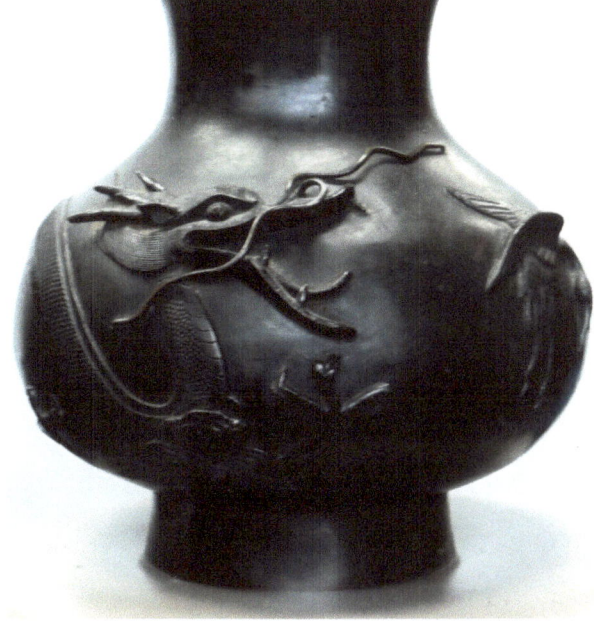

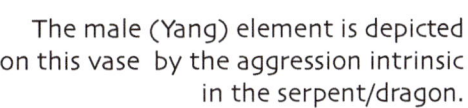

The male (Yang) element is depicted
on this vase by the aggression intrinsic
in the serpent/dragon.

"He may say that he loves you.
Wait and see what he does for you."

-African proverb from Senegal

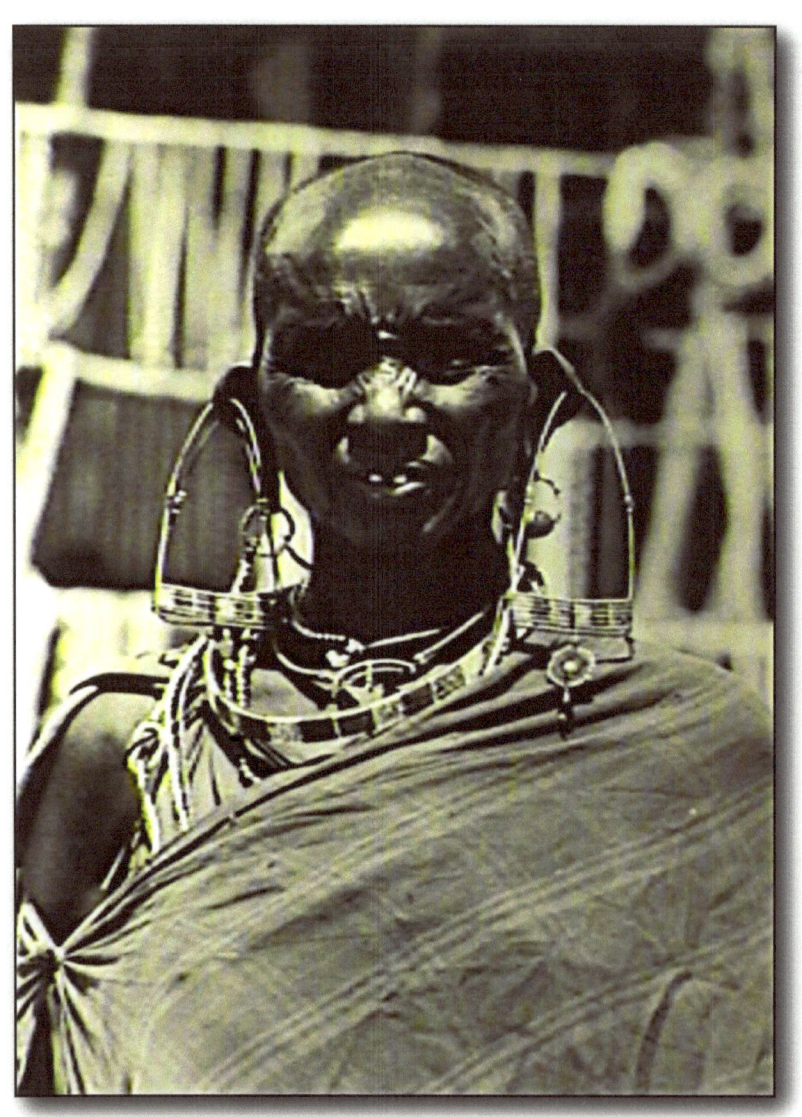

**A Masai woman
and her jewelry**

Photo:
Robert Galloway

"Dine with a stranger,
but save your love for your family."

-African proverb from Ethiopia

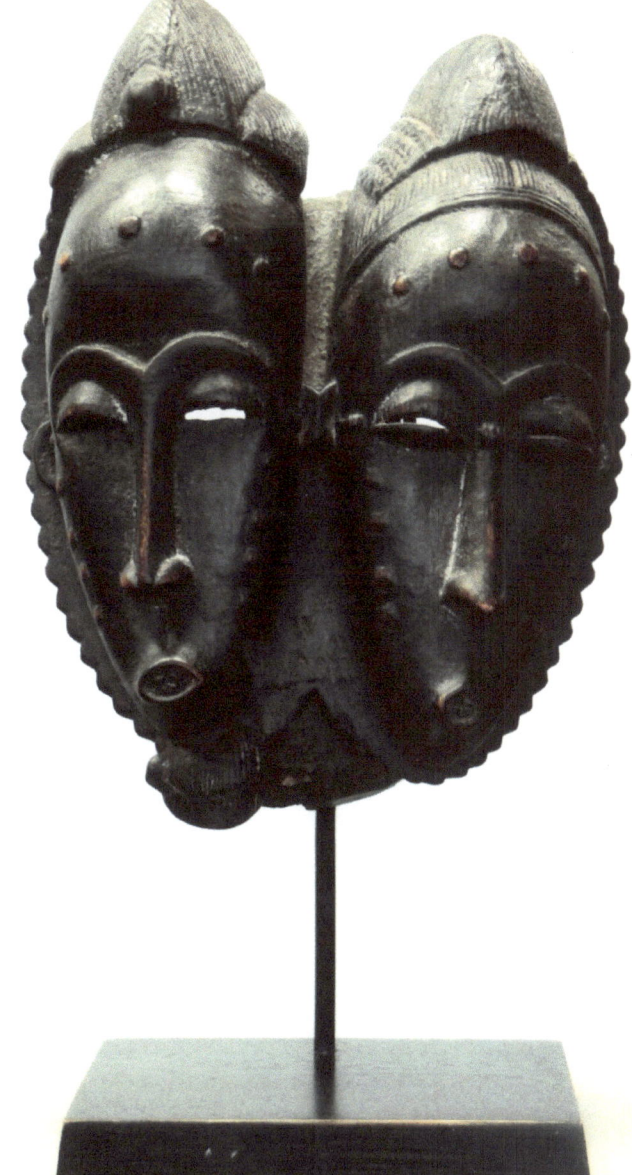

Baule Man and Woman

Their fusion here denotes the
natural unity of man and woman.

"He who marries beauty, marries trouble."

-African proverb from Niger

Wooden Combs

Notice the different symbols on the handle telling stories of value to the owner.

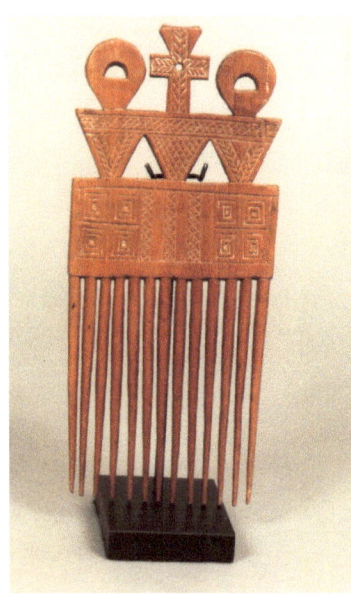

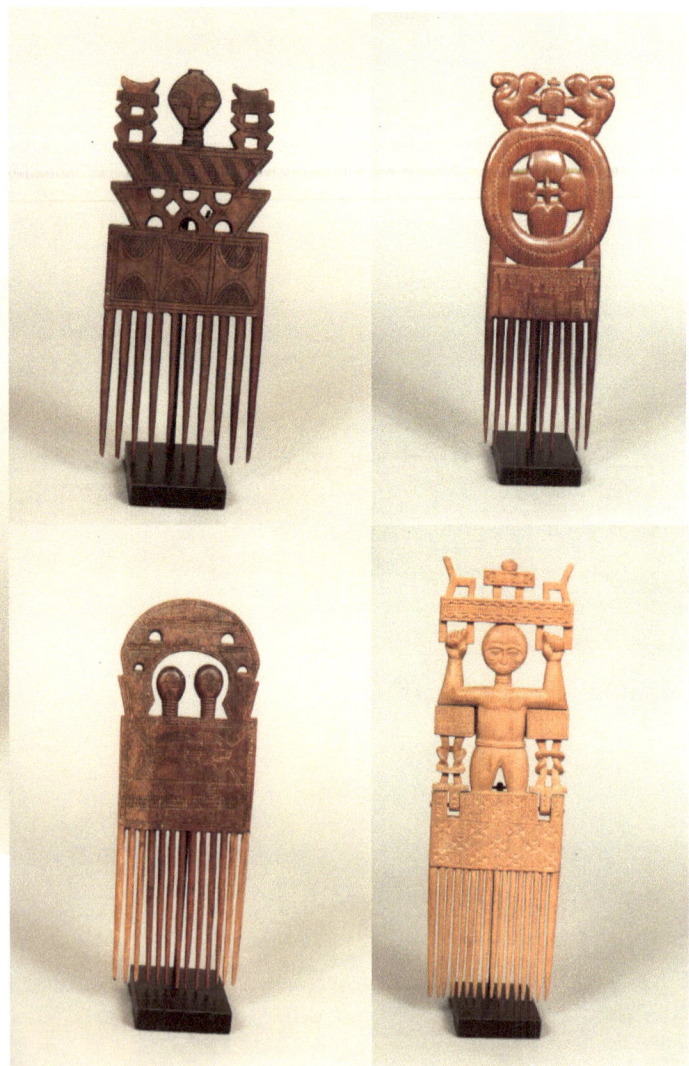

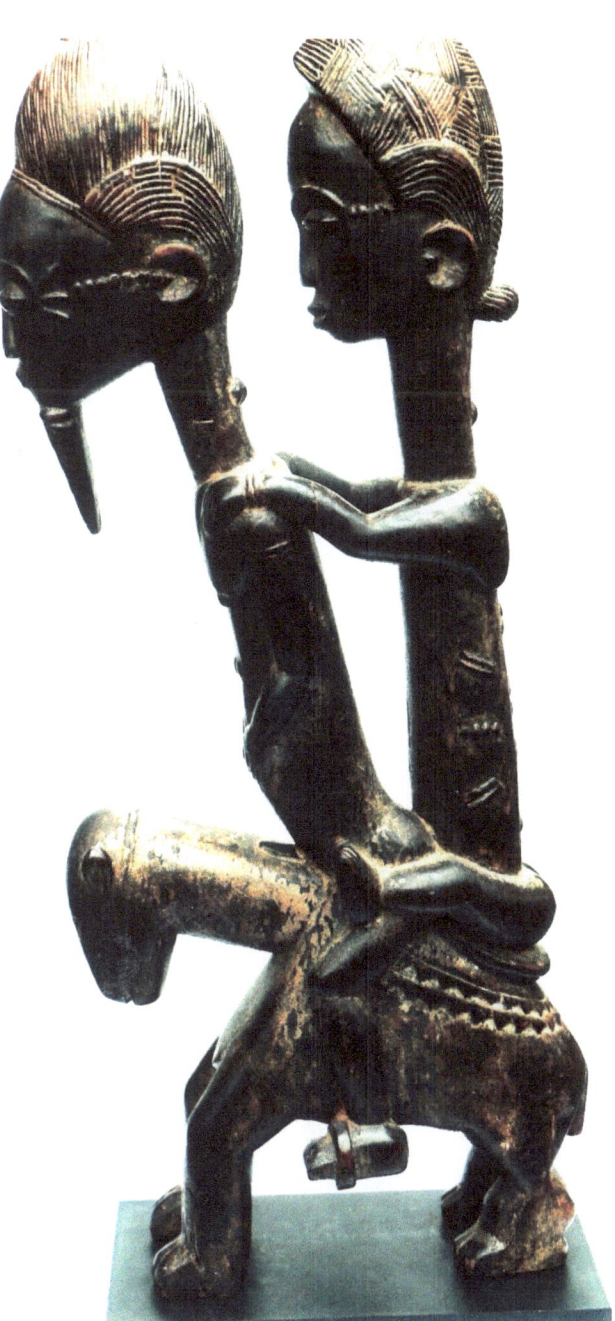

"He who is
being carried
does not know
how far the
town is."

*-African proverb
from Niger*

Baoule Couple
on a Horse

This is from Cote d'Ivoire
(The Ivory Coast).

"An intelligent enemy is better than a stupid friend."

-African proverb from Senegal

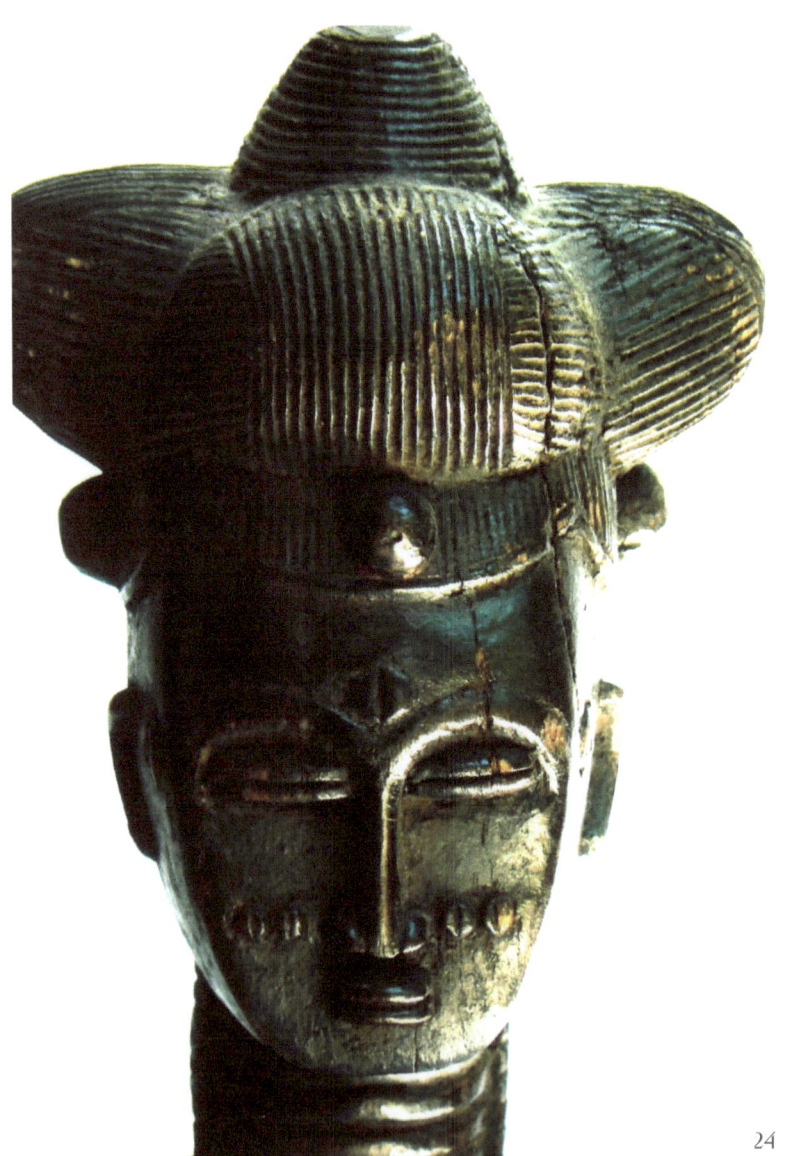

Kuba Woman of Zaire

Her 4 pointed hairdo represents the 4 axis of the universe (north, south, east and west)

The tattoos on her face show her status in the village and the addition of a third eye denotes wisdom and spirituality.

"The toad likes water,
but not when it's boiling"

-African proverb from Ghana

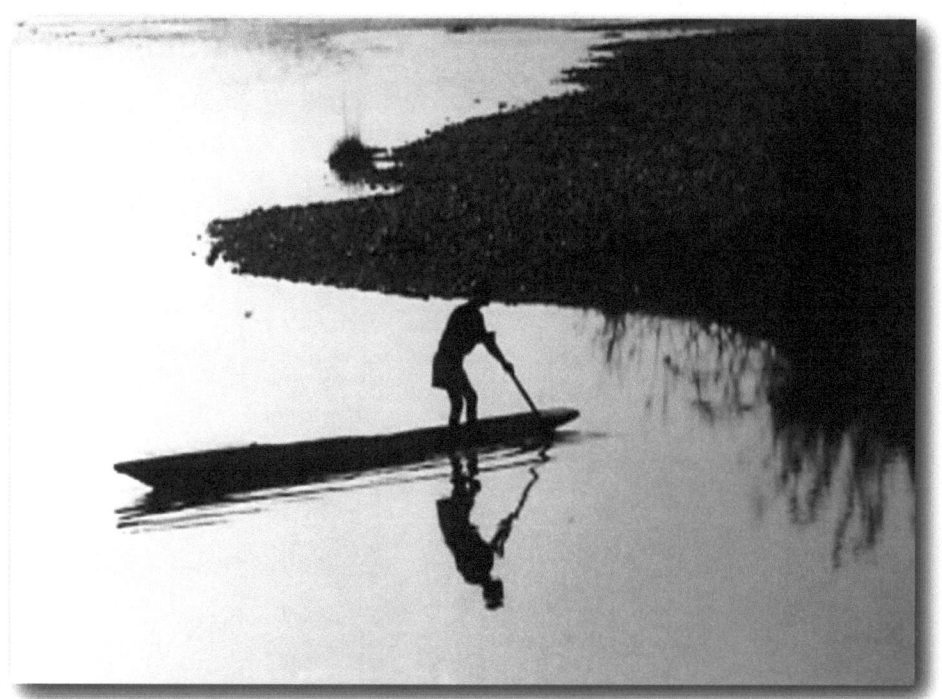

An Anuwak Man on a Boat
Photo: Robert Galloway

This shot was taken moments before a mother hippo attacked his boat
for accidentally coming too close to her babies.

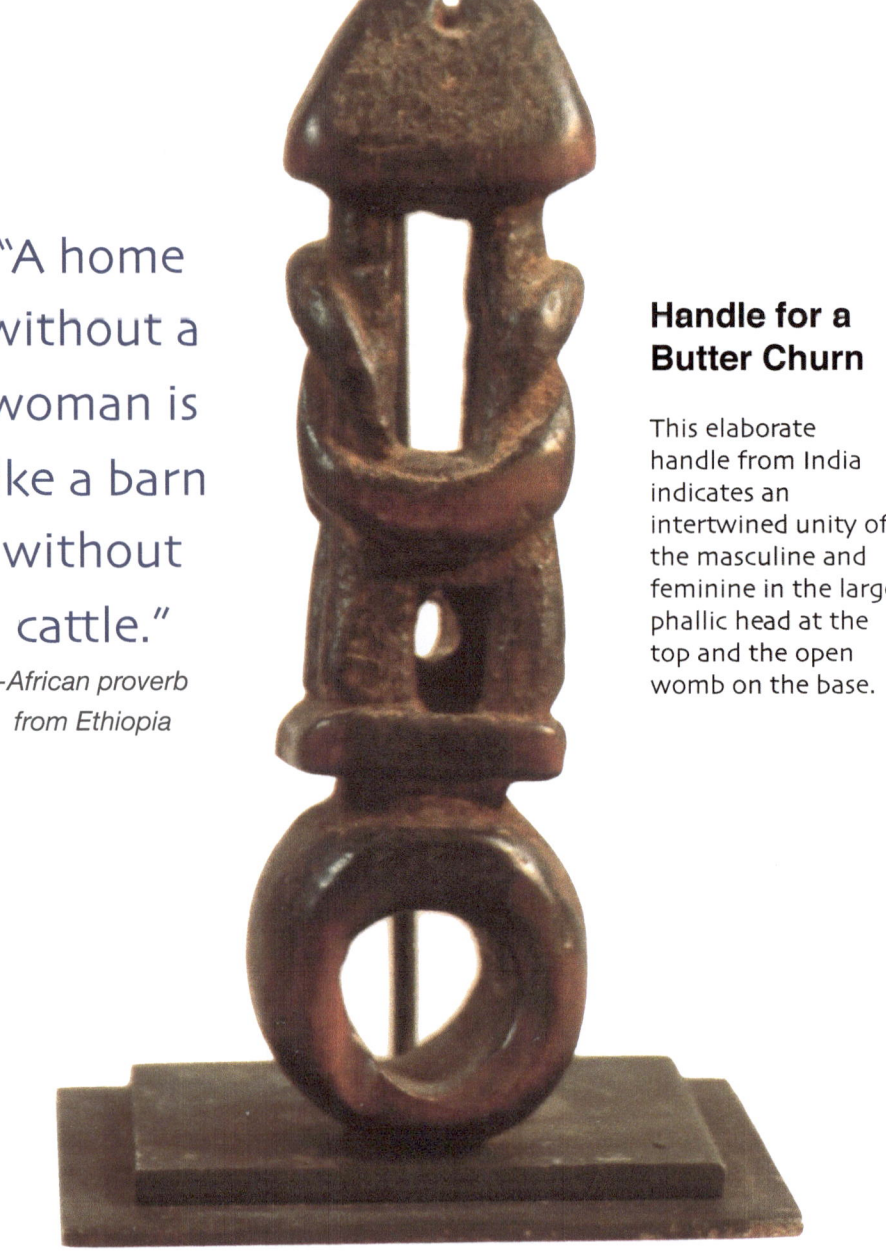

"A home without a woman is like a barn without cattle."

-African proverb from Ethiopia

Handle for a Butter Churn

This elaborate handle from India indicates an intertwined unity of the masculine and feminine in the large phallic head at the top and the open womb on the base.

"The ruin of a nation begins in the homes of its people."

-African proverb from the Ashanti tribe of Ghana

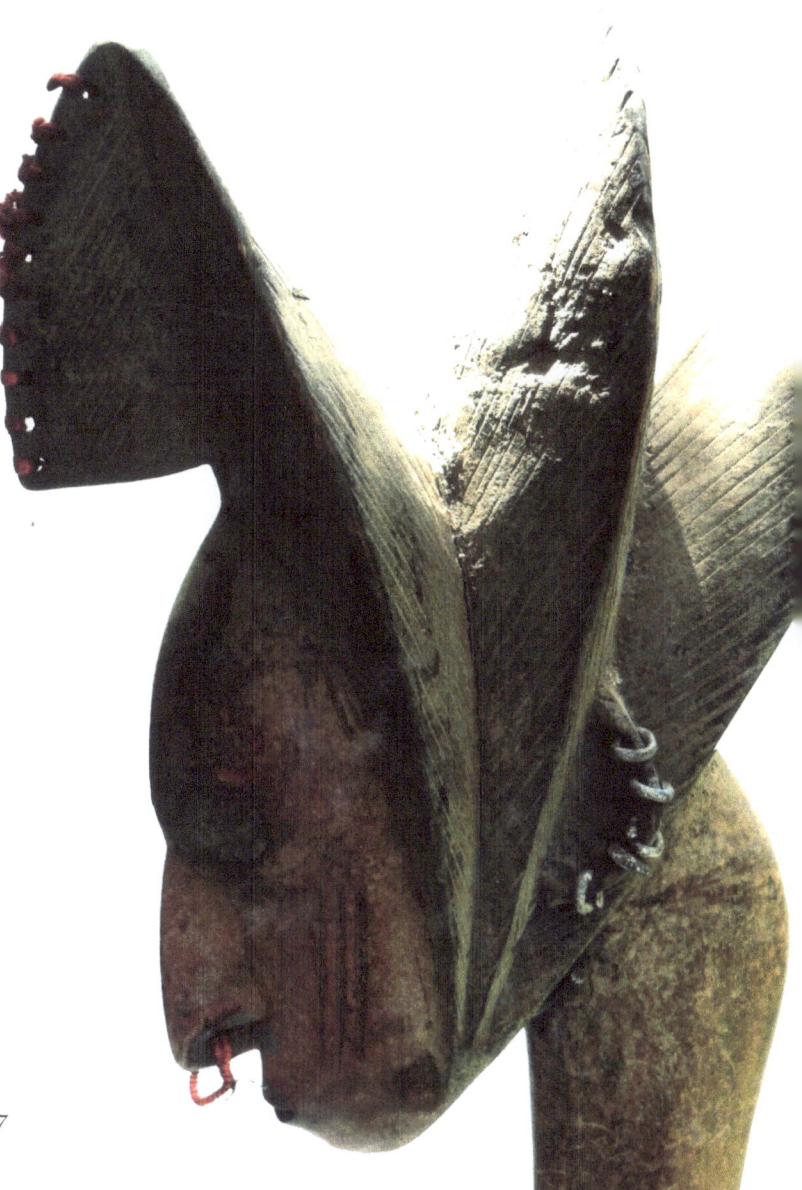

Northern Mali Woman with an Elaborate Hairstyle

This wooden statue depicts a west african woman with a crown-like hairdo and lots of jewelry.

"She is like a road...pretty, but crooked."

-African proverb from Cameroon

27

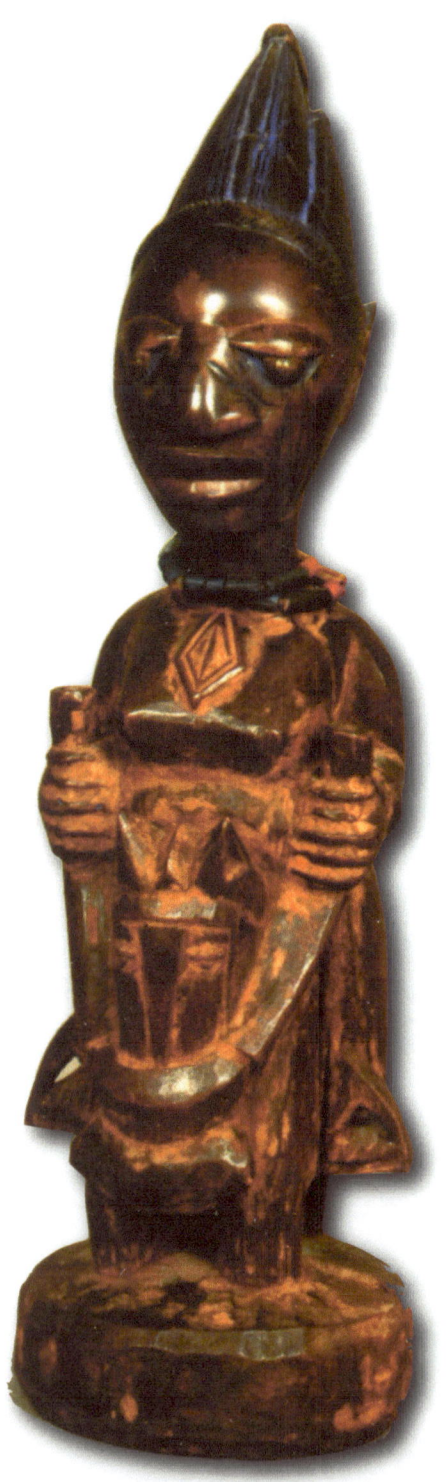

"Do not tell the man who is carrying you that he stinks."

-African proverb from Senegal

Yuroba Soldier on a Horse

Note that the soldier has breasts. It was believed that a good soldier is balanced with male and female qualities.

"To love someone who does not love you is like shaking the tree to see dew drops fall."

-African proverb from Zaire

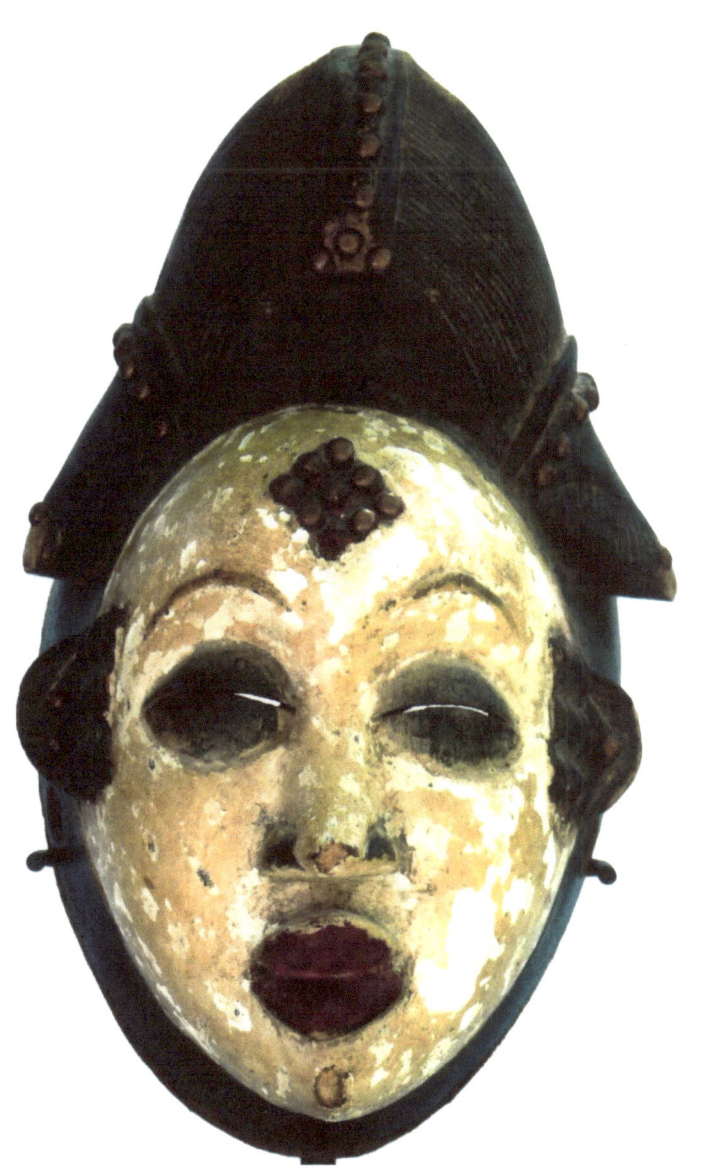

A Punu Mask of Zaire

This mask depicts a woman with a third eye in the middle of her forehead.

The extra eye represents a heightened consciousness-- allowing one to grow spiritually closer to God.

Her hair is shaped like a crown.

Her color is white representing death and an entrance to the spirit world.

"We start as fools and become wise through experience."

-African proverb from Zululand

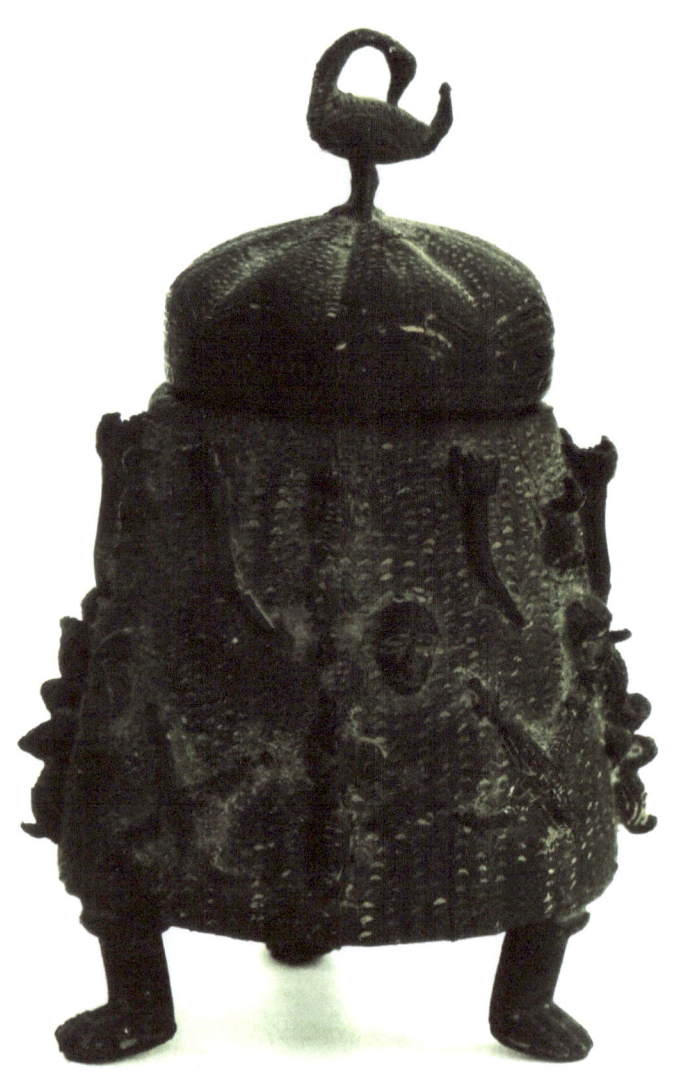

Sankofa Bird Bronze Vessel

The bird on the top of this vase represents a central theme for anyone wanting to maximize their potential.

We stand on the shoulders of giants in our past, but you cannot go forward unless you look back to where you came from.

"Knowledge is better than riches."

-African proverb from Cameroon

Lubas Stool

This distinctive stool from Zaire shows a strong woman supporting whomever chooses to sit on her.

Her large head indicates that she is strong of mind and body-- appropriate for one who is the foundation of the family.

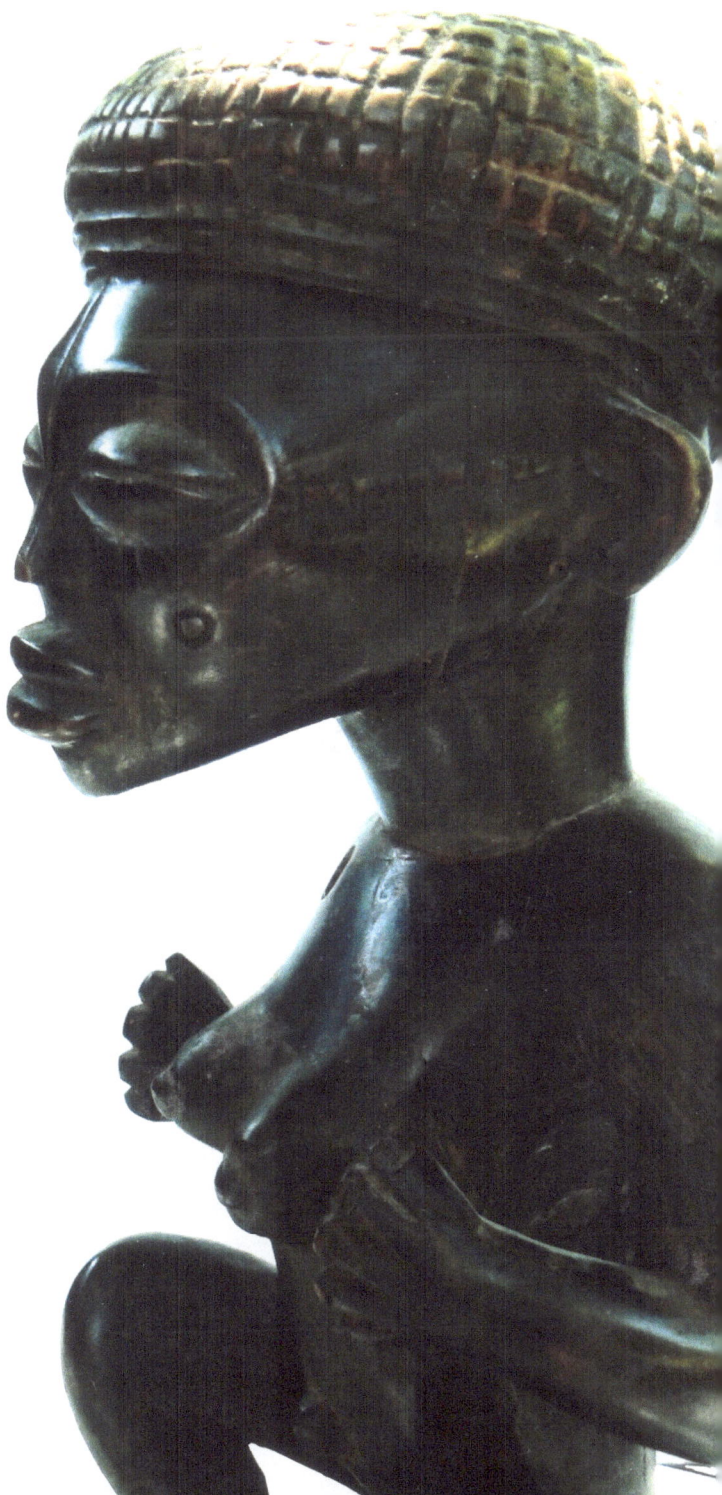

31

"Advise and consul him;
if he does not listen, let adversity teach him."

-African proverb from Ethiopia

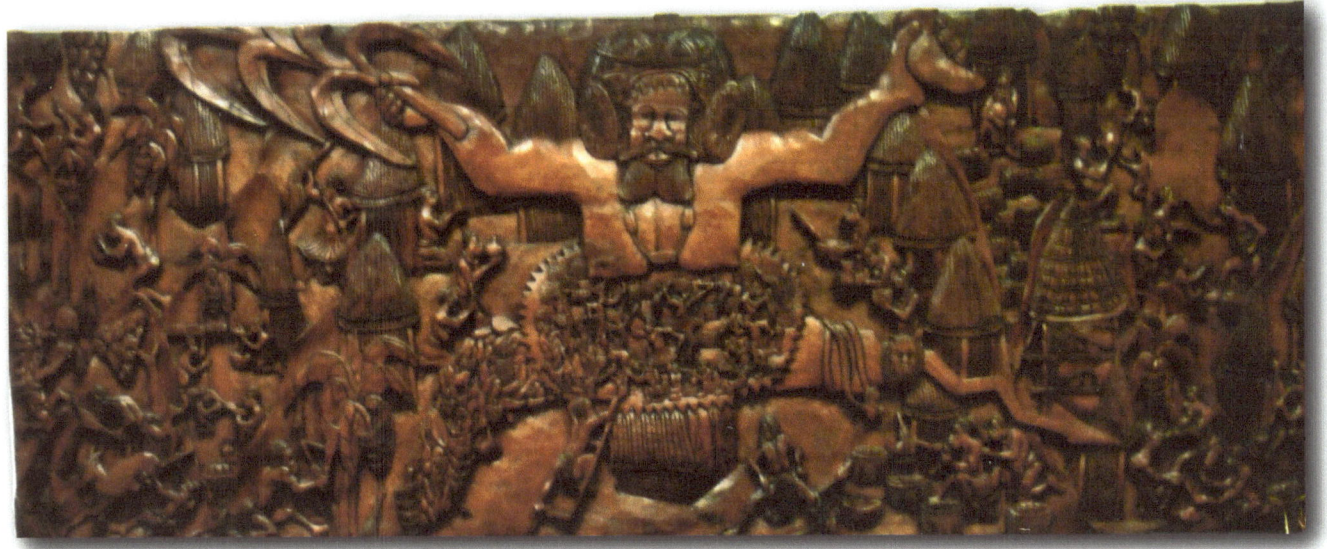

"The Tree of Life"

An intricately carved Haitian piece representing the masculine and feminine of nature. Notice that God is depicted here as both a powerful male and a nurturing female, presiding over a world of both violence and compassionate actions. The stalk of corn represents the sun and a banana the moon in the deity's hands. The sun and the moon correlate to the two genders: the sun being the male and the moon the female. Origin: Haiti

Conclusion:

Know Thyself

"He who learns, teaches."

-African proverb from Ethiopia

Inscribed over the entrance to many ancient tombs and temples, is the message, "KNOW THYSELF."

We live in a wonderful world with almost boundless wealth and plentifulness. In fact, we may have too much. Excessive materialism will obscure the spirit and we are spiritual beings.

In August of 1988, I founded the African American Heritage Museum of Houston. The inspiration for this awesome project attracted the talents of a top-notch Board of Directors. Our board chairman, Dr. Margaret Burroughs, was past president of Chicago's DeSable Museum and chair of the African American Museum Association of America. She was joined by Dr. John Biggers, internationally renown artist; community power brokers Pearl Sewell, Judge Harold Tillman; Councilmember Judson Robinson, Dr. Sarah Trotty, Ada Edwards, Alvia Wardlaw, and art dealer/appraisers Robbie Lee and Eugene Foney.

Our curator, Dr. Carrol Simms was a sculptor and co-director of the Art Department at Texas Southern University and our Docent was Ms. Bettye N. White, who was at that time, secretary to the Texas Southern University Division of Fine Arts.

For over a year, I had devoted considerable time trying to meet Ms. Dominique de Menil, founder of Houston's De Menil Museum...but to no avail. After I founded the African American

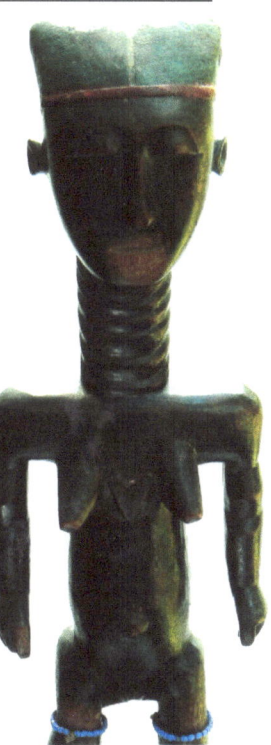

Ashanti Woman
Notice the heart in the center of her chest.

Heritage Museum of Houston, however, she suddenly appeared at my medical practice requesting an impromptu meeting. When I was finally able to sit down with her, she sat patiently through my greeting then smiled radiantly at me, leaned forward and said simply "Dr. Galloway, anything that you need in terms of support for the museum, let me know." She was true to her word, providing fiscal and moral support to the museum's growth and development.

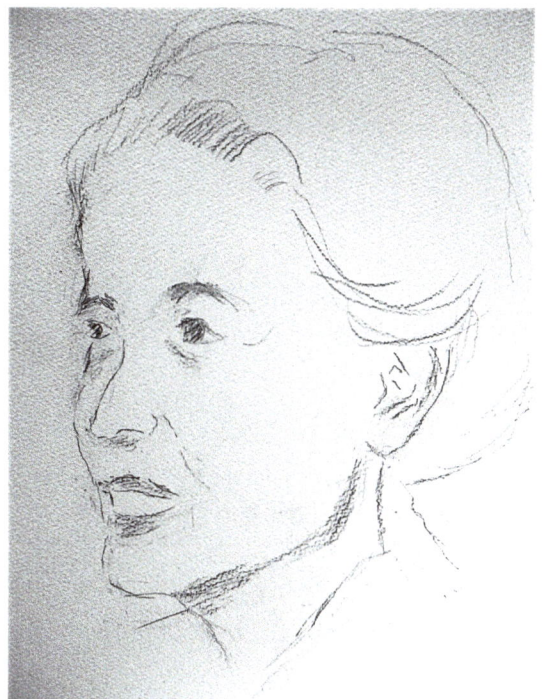

Drawing of Dominique de Menil
by Dr. Robert Galloway

The museum also garnered a number of major supporters including, but not limited to Peter Mazio, Director of the Houston Museum of Fine Arts; Houston Mayor Fred Hofeinz, and Rev. Bill Lawson of Wheeler Avenue Baptist Church.

The African American Heritage Museum of Houston was located in Suite 111A, on the first floor of The St. Joseph's Medical Plaza, a three story professional building at 2101 Crawford Street, across from the St. Josephs Medical Center in Downtown Houston. The Museum was 847 sq. feet with clean white walls which were painted by workers sent from the de Menil Museum. Mrs. de Menil also loaned the Museum pedestals for art objects to be displayed and volunteered advisers for administration events and exhibits.

I recall an incident that occurred during one of our many exhibits. The Museum was presenting a touring photographic exhibition and one Saturday, a man entered, dressed in overhauls, with two small girls. One girl was walking while the man carried the other. They walked to the end of the gallery and paused in front of a portrait of the great American Congresswoman Barbara Jordan.

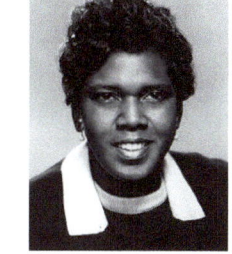

Congresswoman Barbara Jordan
Source: Wikipedia.com

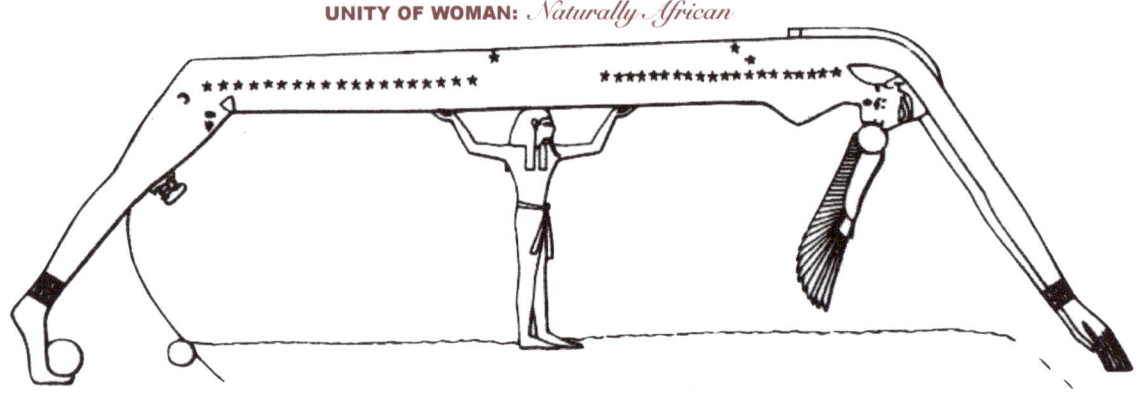

The Goddess Nut Held up by the God Seb

Nut represents the heavens supported by Seb the earth.

One of his daughters asked the man "Who is that daddy?" I sensed a tremendous amount of pride exuding from him as he explained to the children, who Barbara Jordan was. Suddenly, I realized why I had pursued the journey of creating this museum and I felt vindicated in my quest to provide a space where people who looked like me could come, feel not only welcomed, but included in the historic revelations being presented.

From that moment on, I felt even more strongly that all humans are connected as spiritual beings. Though the African American Heritage Museum of Houston existed for only a few years, its creation brought together people of all races and walks of life; allowing us to collectively become ambassadors for culture, unity and tolerance--serving as a catalyst for other such organizations in a future that has proven to be increasingly inclusive.

"Ikenga"

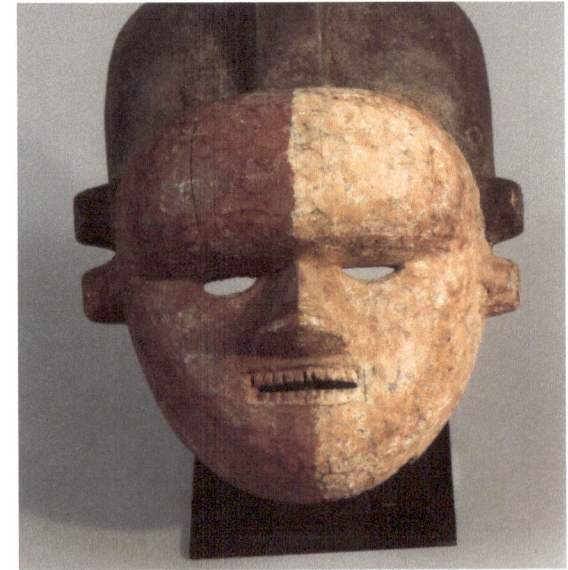

"...That they may be one."

-John 17:21

The international Genome Project has demonstrated that ALL PEOPLE come from Africa. My wife and I were fortunate to have been introduced to the language and cultures of the people of the Nile Rift Valley by both an artist, Dr. John Biggers and an Egyptologist, Dr. Asa Hilliard III. These modern day "griots" taught us to rise above the materialism that can stifle spiritual growth. Theirs was a wisdom which exemplifies the integration of all peoples and the universe. The science of the Genome Project only validates this.

Along the banks of the Nile river are many pyramids . They were all different--some small and others large. That difference was not arbitrary. They were the reflection of the stars along the Milky Way galaxy of which the planet earth is a part.

When we visited Egypt with Dr. Hilliard, we saw hieroglyphics in the temples of Luxor and Abydos. In Abydos, the body of the Goddess "Nut" arched across the ceiling of the temple as a guide for our return to the divine. Life on earth is spent in preparation for the return to heaven...Woman represents that heaven.

Perhaps the perspectives of ancient Egypt should to be the gold standard for humankind today. That would be a way to raise ourselves above the immense materialism in which we are all submerged.

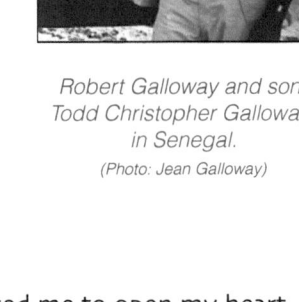

Robert Galloway and son Todd Christopher Galloway in Senegal.
(Photo: Jean Galloway)

I feel that my travels and actions over the past decades, finding and embracing my past, my culture and my humanity has allowed me to open my heart, mind and spirit to light, life and love.

I know now that feeling and knowing is food for the soul and we all have a duty to use our journey to benefit all humanity. I know we are driven to use our gifts to achieve our ultimate goal of reunion with our creator....no matter how long it takes.

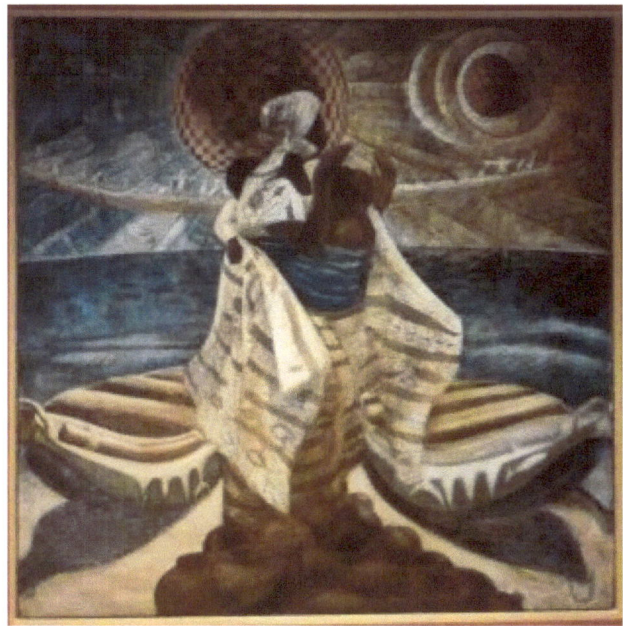

Woman with twins and two boats - John Biggers

The purpose of this book is to empower young people to recognize their potential and blossom like children of God. Before they do so, they must reflect upon the meaning of the adage, "Sankofa" : "You cannot go forward unless you first look back where you came from."

We encourage you, dear reader, to visit Africa sometime in your life, if for no reason than to see where all races have come from and to reconnect with the essence of our spirituality. Only then can you know yourself and move forward.

This advice is especially true for young women who must recognize WHO THEY ARE if civilization is to progress.

As demonstrated numerous times in this book, the female is the center for the home, the community, the society...the very foundation of all humanity. Like the ancient goddess Nut, she must embrace her value and role in connecting humankind to the heavens.

After all, it is OUR legacy.

www.ingramcontent.com/pod-product-compliance
Lightning Source LLC
Chambersburg PA
CBHW050403180526
45159CB00005B/2130